1 Introduction

A fundamental result of agency theory is the trade-off between risk and incentives (Holmstrom (1979); Shavell (1979)). An implication of the theory is that the more variation there is in firm profits, the less use of profit sharing there should be. If employees are risk-averse, then greater variation in firm profits makes contracts based on firm profits more costly. Therefore, when we look at CEO contracts we should see a negative relationship between variation in firm profits and the proportion of CEO pay that varies with firm profits. Surprisingly, this is not what we find and there is some evidence that the opposite is true (Core and Guay (2002)).[1] This paper presents a theoretical model that suggests the reason for the lack of empirical support is that CEOs have discretion with regards to the tasks they perform. The paper empirically analyzes contracts given to employees in British manufacturing firms. The paper finds that for production workers who do not have discretion over the tasks that they do, the use of profit sharing is negatively related to variation in firm profits. However, for managers and production workers *with* discretion, the use of profit sharing is *positively* related to variation in firm profits.

The paper theoretically analyzes the implications of giving the agent discretion. Consider a production line worker who has been given discretion on how fast the production line will run. The worker observes private information about the number of errors that are occurring on the line. The firm would like the worker to slow the line once the number of errors gets above a certain level. There is an incentive problem because the worker would like to slow the line irrespective of the number of errors! That is, the worker would always prefer to have the line run slow because it is easier. So by giving the worker this option, the firm creates an incentive problem. In the language of the adverse selection problem, the worker always wants to pretend to be a "lots of errors on the line" type. To solve the adverse selection problem,

---

[1] See Prendergast (1999) for a detailed discussion of the empirical work on different aspects of agency theory. Also see Aggarwal and Samwick (1999) and Aggarwal and Samwick (2002).

the firm can use an "input" contract. This is a contract where the firm hires a supervisor to observe information about the number of errors occurring on the line (assume that the worker's choice to slow the line is perfectly observed by the firm). Alternatively, the firm can use an "output" contract. This is a contract that pays the worker as a function of firm profits. The relative value of using firm profits is a function of the relative noisiness of firm profits as a signal of the worker's private information. If uncertainty takes the form of variation in the demand for the firm's products, then it is likely to increase the variation in firm profits. However, it is also likely to affect the production line and the noisiness of the supervisor's information on the number of errors occurring on the line. If variation in demand affects the latter more than the former, the firm will switch to giving the worker profit sharing. In this case, the model predicts that for workers with discretion, there will be a positive relationship between variation in firm profits and the use of profit sharing.

The paper empirically analyzes contracts given to employees in British manufacturing firms. As a first approximation the paper analyzes contracts given to managers and contracts given to production line workers. The results show that for managers there is a positive (but not statistically significant) relationship between variation in demand and the use of profit sharing. For production line workers there is a negative (but not statistically significant) relationship between variation in demand and the use of profit sharing. This suggest that discretion plays an important role. One concern is that some of the workers also have discretion. The paper analyzes the sub-sample of workers that report that they have no discretion over the tasks that they do. For this sub-sample, there is the predicted negative relationship between variation in demand and the use of profit sharing.

The paper then analyzes the firm's decision to give production line workers discretion over the tasks that these workers do. The empirical model accounts for the simultaneous choice to give a worker discretion and profit sharing. Further, the model allows the choice of profit sharing to depend on worker discretion. The results show that for workers that do not have discretion, there is a negative relationship between variation in demand and the use of profit sharing. For workers with discretion, there is a positive relationship between variation in demand and the use of profit sharing. The results show that there is a trade-off between risk and incentives. However, when agents have discretion uncertainty in the environment, may reduce the ability of the principal to monitor the agent, forcing the use of output or profit sharing contracts.

Unlike this paper, Holmstrom (1979) and Shavell (1979) model a situation where the agent does not have discretion. A risk-averse agent must choose the level of "effort" to expend on a single task. The agent's effort level is unobserved by the principal. An implication of this model is that an optimal contract will place less weight on the noisier measures of the agent's effort choice. Three explanations have been given for why the empirical evidence does not support the theory. First, in relation to CEO pay, the use of profit sharing may have less to do with incentives and more to do with labor markets.[2] Second, the empirical tests may not have accounted for the risk preferences of the agent. Serfes (2002) analyzes a theoretical model where agents have differing risk preferences and they have the ability to match with principals facing differing levels of uncertainty. Ackerberg and Botticini (2002) account for this issue in their analysis of contract choice amongst tenant farmers in Renaissance Tuscany. Third, and the one presented and tested in this paper, is that the agents we observe, in particular CEOs, have a substantial amount of discretion.

In general, CEO contracts allow them to observe private information and make choices contingent upon that information. Consider a CEO's decision to build a factory in Peru. Shareholders allow the CEO to build the factory if the building of the factory will lead to a greater return on their stock. Prior to making the decision, the CEO observes information on the distribution of returns to building the factory. Given that information, she makes her decision. The shareholders observe that the factory was or was not built, but they do not observe the information that was available to the CEO. If the CEO's preferences in regards to building the factory are different from the preferences of the stock holders, then there is an adverse selection problem.[3]

---

[2]See for example Oyer (2002).

[3]See Myerson (1982, 1985) for a discussion of mechanisms where the principal contracts

Assumption	Adams	Core & Qian	Prendergast
Risk-averse agent	√	√	
Private information	√	√	√
Private costs in task choice	√	√	√
Cost of effort within task			√
Mean/variance returns		√	√
Costly private information		√	
Contract on firm output	√	√	√
Contract on task choice	√		√
Contract on private information	√		

Table 1: Assumptions of Agent Discretion Models

The principal (shareholder, supervisor, franchiser) may not know *why* an action was taken by the agent (CEO, worker, franchisee), even when they know *what* action was taken.[4]

It is not immediately clear what effect the adverse selection problem has the relationship between risk and incentives. However, it is clear that using data on contracts in which agents have discretion is not a fair test of the Holmstrom/Shavell model. The empirical results presented below show that for agents without discretion, there is a trade-off between risk and incentives. Accounting for the missing variable of agent discretion, provides evidence in support of the theory. Apart from this paper, there are two papers (Core and Qian (2001) and Prendergast (2002a)) that theoretically analyze the incentive problem when the agent has discretion. See Table 1 for a comparison of each model's assumptions and Table 2 for a comparison of each model's prediction.

Core and Qian (2001) consider the incentive problem for CEOs. In their model the agent must choose between different tasks and can obtain private information on the value of those tasks. However, obtaining this information is costly to the agent and beneficial to the principal. Moreover, different

---

on signals of both the agent's private action and the agent's private information. Myerson calls these generalized principal-agent problems.

[4] I am paraphrasing Core and Qian (2001).

Model	Predictions
Adams	If discretion, uncertainty implies profit sharing.
Core & Qian	Uncertainty implies high powered incentives.
Prendergast	Uncertainty implies discretion and profit sharing.

Table 2: Predictions of Agent Discretion Models

tasks have different risk profiles and the agent is more risk-averse than the principal. The authors show that greater uncertainty increases the value to the principal of having the agent obtain this private information. As the principal can only contract on signals of the firm's profits, to motivate the agent to obtain her private information, the principal must increase the power of the incentives. In this way, uncertainty leads to contracts that place greater weight on firm profits.

Prendergast (2002a) considers a situation in which the principal must decide whether or not to give the agent discretion. If the agent does not have discretion, then the problem is similar to the one analyzed by Holmstrom (1979) and Shavell (1979). However, when the agent has discretion the agent must choose effort levels over multiple tasks (similar to Holmstrom and Milgrom (1991)). The agent's choice depends on the agent's private information. As the principal is assumed to be only able to contract on signals of the agent's task choice, effort level and firm profits, there is a "multi-tasking" problem which can only be solved by contracting on firm profits. Uncertainty enters the model by increasing the value of the agent's private information and thus increasing the value of giving the agent discretion.

Unlike Prendergast (2002a) the model presented below only considers the case where the agent has discretion. The other important difference between the model presented below and the previous work, is that the principal can contract on signals of the agent's private information (other than firm profits). Uncertainty enters the model by affecting the noisiness of these signals. If uncertainty makes these signals less valuable than firm profits, the principal will switch to using firm profits.

The empirical results presented below give some varied support for the implications of the model presented in Prendergast (2002a). In particular, the results show that uncertainty leads to greater agent discretion and greater use of profit sharing. However, it is not the case that agent discretion automatically implies profit sharing. Further, it is not the case that the two practices are always complements. The empirical results give support to the implications of the theoretical model presented below. For workers without discretion, uncertainty leads to less use of profit sharing. For workers with discretion, uncertainty seems to have greater affect on the firm's ability to monitor the worker's private information than it has on variation in firm profits. For workers with discretion, uncertainty leads to greater use of profit sharing. Unfortunately, the data is not detailed enough to test the implications of the model presented in Core and Qian (2001).

The paper continues as follows. Section 2 presents the adverse selection problem and the theoretical results. Section 3 discusses the data, which is based on surveys of a large number of manufacturing employees and the manufacturing establishments that they work for. Section 4 presents the results. Section 5 concludes.

2 The Model and Hypotheses

This section presents a model which formalizes agent discretion and how it impacts the incentive problem. The model analyzes the incentive problem associated with the task choice (adverse selection) and assumes that there is no effort level incentive problem (moral hazard). Proposition 1 states that conditional on the worker having discretion, the firm places greater value on profit sharing when it is more difficult to monitor the worker's private information. Proposition 2 states that conditional on the worker having discretion, if uncertainty has a greater affect on the ability of the firm to monitor the worker's information than it does on firm profits, greater uncertainty is associated with greater use of profit sharing.

2.1 Adverse Selection

The model consists of two players, a firm (the principal) and a worker (the agent). The firm offers the worker a binding contract, which describes the task the worker will choose and how the worker will be paid. The worker either accepts or rejects the firm's contract offer given a common *ex ante* belief about the state of the world. The value of the worker's outside option is 0. If he accepts the contract, the worker then observes his private information regarding the state of the world and chooses a task. The firm is risk neutral and the worker is risk averse with a utility function that is separable in money, $u : \Re^2 \to \Re$, such that $u(\pi, e) = v(\pi) - e$, $v(0) = 0$, $v' > 0$ and $v'' < 0$, where π is the monetary payment and e is the "effort" cost of the task chosen.

The following time line summarizes the model:

1. The firm and worker have a common belief regarding the state ($s \in \{0, 1\}$, $f = \Pr(s = 1)$).

2. The firm makes a take-it-or-leave-it contract offer, $\{t(W_s), \pi(t, F_s, r)\}$, where $t \in \{0, 1\}$ is the worker's task choice, $W_s \in \{0, 1\}$ is the worker's signal of the state, $F_s \in \{0, 1\}$ is the firm's signal of the state, $r \in \{0, 1\}$ is the firm's revenue, and $\pi \in \Re$ is the payment to the worker.

3. The worker accepts or rejects the contract offer.

4. The worker observes a signal of the state W_s, and updates his belief regarding the state ($f_1 = \Pr(s = 1 | W_s = 1)$ and $f_0 = \Pr(s = 1 | W_s = 0)$, such that $f_1 > f_0$). Let $\sigma = \Pr(s = 1 | W_s = 1) = \Pr(s = 0 | W_s = 0)$, such that $0.5 < \sigma < 1$.

5. The worker chooses a task $t(W_s)$, knowing that the cost of $t = 1$ is greater than the cost of $t = 0$ by the amount $e > 0$.

6. The firm observes t and F_s, receives revenue r and pays the worker $\pi(t, F_s, r)$. However, the payment scheme is either based on t and F_s,

or the payment scheme is based on r, and not any other combination. Let $\phi = \Pr(s=1|F_s=1) = \Pr(s=0|F_s=0)$, such that $0.5 < \phi < 1$.

The worker's information has value to the firm because the firm's stochastic revenue (r) has a distribution that depends on both the task chosen by the worker and the state of the world. The probability distribution can be written as follows.

$$\Pr(r=1|t,s) = \begin{array}{ll} p_0 & \text{if } t=0, \\ p_1 & \text{if } t=1, s=1, \\ 1-p_1 & \text{if } t=1, s=0 \end{array} \quad (1)$$

where $p_1 > p_0 > 1 - p_1$. The firm can get greater expected revenue by asking the worker to choose task $t=1$, however this is only true if the state $s=1$. If the state $s=0$ then the firm's expected revenue is greater when it asks the worker to choose $t=0$. The firm also observes information about the state of the world denoted F_s. However, this information is assumed to be received "too late" to be valuable for decision making, although this information may still be "early" enough to be useful for monitoring the worker's decision making. Figure 1 represents the expected return of each task given the firm and the worker's common *ex ante* belief f that the state $s=1$. The figure and Equation (1) represent the fact that if the worker chooses task $t=0$, then the probability of $r=1$ is *independent of the state* and equal to p_0. If the worker chooses $t=1$ the expected return depends upon the state and is higher (p_1) if the state is $s=1$ and lower ($1-p_1$) if the state is $s=0$.

Consider the case where the firm gives the worker discretion, and in particular the firm prefers that the worker choose $t=1$ if $W_s=1$ and $t=0$ if $W_s=0$.[5] This is an adverse selection problem where the IR constraint is *ex ante* rather than an interim constraint. The firm has two choices, it can use an input contract or an output contract. These contracts are modelled simply as different signals.

---

[5]See Adams (2003) for a more detailed analysis of this model.

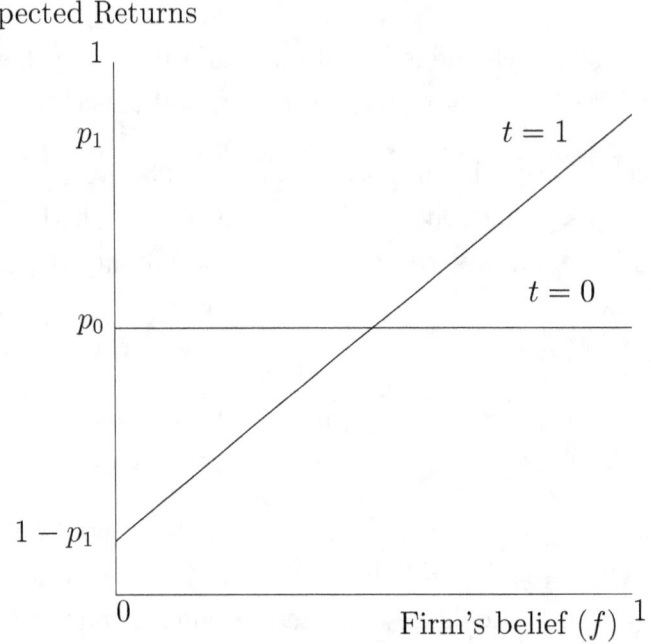

Figure 1: Expected Returns to the Firm Given Belief of s

If an input contract is used the firm's problem is

$$\max_{\pi(t,F_s)} \quad (1 - f \cdot \sigma)(p_0 - (\phi \cdot f_0 \pi(0,1) + (1 - \phi \cdot f_0)\pi(0,0)))$$
$$+ f \cdot \sigma(f_1 \cdot p_1 - ((1 - \phi \cdot f_1)\pi(1,0) + \phi \cdot f_1 \pi(1,1)))$$

s.t.

$(IC0)$ $\quad \phi \cdot f_0 v(\pi(0,1)) + (1 - \phi \cdot f_0)v(\pi(0,0))$
$\quad \geq (1 - \phi \cdot f_0)v(\pi(1,0)) + \phi \cdot f_0 v(\pi(1,1)) - e \quad (2)$

$(IC1)$ $\quad (1 - \phi \cdot f_1)v(\pi(1,0)) + \phi \cdot f_1 v(\pi(1,1)) - e$
$\quad \geq \phi \cdot f_1 v(\pi(0,1)) + (1 - \phi \cdot f_1)v(\pi(0,0))$

(IR) $\quad (1 - f \cdot \sigma)(\phi \cdot f_0 v(\pi(0,1)) + (1 - \phi \cdot f_0)v(\pi(0,0)))$
$\quad + f \cdot \sigma((1 - \phi \cdot f_1)v(\pi(1,0)) + \phi \cdot f_1 v(\pi(1,1)) - e) \geq 0$

where the notation $f \cdot \sigma = (1 - f)(1 - \sigma) + f\sigma$, and it is assumed that $\Pr(F_s = 1|W_s = 1) = \Pr(F_s = 0|W_s = 0) = (1 - \phi)(1 - \sigma) + \phi\sigma$. The worker's supervisor does not directly monitor the worker's information, but uses his own *independent* observation of the circumstances to decide on the reasonableness of the worker's decision.

Alternatively, the principal may offer a profit sharing contract, $\pi(r)$, in which case the firm's problem is

$$\max_{\pi(r)} \ (1 - f \cdot \sigma)(p_0 - ((1-p_0)\pi(0) + p_0\pi(1)))$$
$$+ f \cdot \sigma(f_1 \cdot p_1 - ((1 - f_1 \cdot p_1)\pi(0) + f_1 \cdot p_1\pi(1)))$$

s.t.

$(IC0)$ $\quad (1-p_0)v(\pi(0)) + p_0 v(\pi(1))$
$\quad \geq (1 - f_0 \cdot p_1)v(pi(0)) + f_0 \cdot p_1 v(\pi(1)) - e$ (3)

$(IC1)$ $\quad (1 - f_1 \cdot p_1)v(\pi(0)) + f_1 \cdot p_1 v(\pi(1)) - e$
$\quad \geq (1-p_0)v(\pi(0)) + p_0 v(\pi(1))$

(IR) $\quad (1 - f \cdot \sigma)((1-p_0)v(\pi(0)) + p_0 v(\pi(1)))$
$\quad + f \cdot \sigma((1 - f_1 \cdot p_1)v(\pi(0)) + f_1 \cdot p_1 v(\pi(1)) - e) \geq 0$

The following propositions show how the relative value of the input and output contracts change with the parameters of the model. The value to the firm of each type of contract is denoted V_{DP}, where $D \in \{0,1\}$ denotes agent discretion and $P \in \{0,1\}$ denotes profit sharing.

Proposition 1 states that conditional on the worker having descretion, as the accuracy of the firm's signal of the state falls, the value of the profit sharing contract increases relative to the value of the monitoring contract.

Proposition 1 *Given the assumptions stated above for all $\phi \in (.5, 1)$*

$$\frac{\partial(V_{11} - V_{10})}{\partial \phi} < 0 \qquad (4)$$

Proof. See appendix.

When the worker has discretion, the firm only wants the worker to choose the difficult task ($t = 1$) when the worker's information suggests that the state is $s = 1$. Thus the incentive scheme aims to reward matching the task $t = 1$ with the state $s = 1$ and punish mismatching. Therefore, when ϕ is high, there is less noise in the incentive scheme, reducing the risk borne by the worker and the cost of the incentive scheme to the principal.

What is not clear from Proposition 1 is how uncertainty affects the firm's choice of contract. In particular, uncertainty related to fluctuations in demand for the firm's product may affect both noise associated with the firm's signal of the state (ϕ) and the noise associated with the firm's revenue. Let δ represent this common noise parameter, and

$$2\phi \cdot f_1 - 1 = \alpha\delta \tag{5}$$

and

$$f_1 \cdot p_1 - p_0 = \beta\delta \tag{6}$$

where $\alpha, \beta \in [0,1]$. The following proposition states that if the uncertainty affects the firm's signal of the worker's private information more than it affects the firm's signal of profits, then greater uncertainty leads to greater use of output contracts. Similarly, if uncertainty affects the signal of firm revenue more, greater uncertainty leads to great use of input contracts.

Proposition 2 *Given the assumptions stated above and assuming $(1 - f \cdot \sigma)p_0 + f \cdot \sigma(f_1 \cdot p_1)$ remains constant, then for all $\delta \in (0,1)$*

1. *If $\alpha > \beta$, then $\frac{\partial(V_{11}-V_{10})}{\partial \delta} < 0$*

2. *If $\alpha < \beta$, then $\frac{\partial(V_{11}-V_{10})}{\partial \delta} > 0$*

Proof. See appendix.

Greater uncertainty is associated with more noise and a lower δ. If α is greater than β, the change in δ has greater effect on monitoring as a signal of the agent's information than it has on revenue as a signal of the agent's information. Under this circumstance, greater uncertainty lead to greater use of profit sharing.

2.2 Linear Latent Profit Model

There exist four possible contracts, the latent value of each is presented below. First, the value of neither delegating decision making nor using profit sharing is denoted by A_{ij} for worker i and firm j. The latent profits of the other contracts will be compared to this one.

$$V_{00} = A_{ij} \tag{7}$$

The value of delegating decision making but not using profit sharing is V_{10}. The relative value of this contract may be a function of the measure of uncertainty $X_{j\delta}$, of other characteristics of the worker (X_i), and of the firm (X_j). Note that in the theoretical model higher δ is associated with *less* uncertainty, in this section X_δ is associated with *more* uncertainty. Value is also affected by unobservable characteristics of the worker and firm (ϵ_{ijD}).

$$V_{10} = A_{ij} + X_{j\delta}\beta_{\delta D} + X_i\beta_{iD} + X_j\beta_{jD} + \epsilon_{ijD} \tag{8}$$

The value of using profit sharing but not delegating decision making is V_{01}.

$$V_{01} = A_{ij} + X_{j\delta}\beta_{\delta P} + X_i\beta_{iP} + X_j\beta_{jP} + \epsilon_{ijP} \tag{9}$$

where ϵ_{ijP} represents unobservable characteristics that affect the relative value of the contract with profit sharing only. The other variables are defined above. The value of delegating decision making and also using profit sharing is V_{11}.

$$\begin{aligned}V_{11} = &A_{ij} + X_{j\delta}\beta_{\delta D} + X_i\beta_{iD} + X_j\beta_{jD} + \epsilon_{ijD} \\ &+ X_{j\delta}\beta_{\delta P} + X_i\beta_{iP} + X_j\beta_{jP} + \epsilon_{ijP} \\ &+ X_{j\delta}\beta_{\delta DP} + X_i\beta_{iDP} + X_j\beta_{jDP} + \epsilon_{ijDP}\end{aligned} \tag{10}$$

Note that the β_{DP} coefficients determine the "extra" value of having both practices together.

2.3 Hypotheses

Holmstrom (1979), Shavell (1979), Prendergast (2002a) and the model presented above, suggest four hypotheses that can be tested using the data set presented below. The first two are based on results from Prendergast (2002a). The first is that uncertainty leads firms to give workers more discretion. The second is that discretion implies profit sharing. The third hypothesis is based on Holmstrom (1979) and Shavell (1979). It states that if the employee has no discretion, then uncertainty leads to less use of profit sharing. The fourth hypothesis is based on the model presented above. It states that if the employee has discretion and uncertainty has greater affect on monitoring as a signal of the worker's private information, then uncertainty will lead to a greater use of profit sharing.

The model presented in Prendergast (2002a) implies the following hypothesis. The hypothesis states that the value of giving both the employee discretion and profit sharing increases with uncertainty. Following from Equation (10), the hypothesis is as follows.

Hypothesis 1 *Uncertainty and Discretion*
$\frac{\partial V_{11}}{\partial X_{j\delta}} = \beta_{\delta D} + \beta_{\delta P} + \beta_{\delta DP} > 0$

The second hypothesis implied by Prendergast (2002a) is that firms must use profit sharing when discretion is used. A weaker version is that the two practices are complements. The value to the firm of the two choices is supermodular in the two choices if, $V_{00} + V_{11} > V_{01} + V_{10}$ (Milgrom and Roberts (1990)). It is straight forward, to see that the following hypothesis is implied by supermodularity. If this result holds, then in general the firm will use profit sharing with discretion.

Hypothesis 2 *Supermodularity*
$X_{j\delta}\beta_{\delta DP} + X_i\beta_{iDP} + X_j\beta_{jDP} > 0$

The Holmostrom/Shavell result implies the following hypothesis. The hypothesis states that conditional on the worker having no decision making power, greater uncertainty will lead to a reduction in the value of profit sharing. The appropriate difference is

$$V_{01} - V_{00} = X_{j\delta}\beta_{\delta P} + X_i\beta_{iP} + X_j\beta_{jP} + \epsilon_{ijP} \qquad (11)$$

Therefore, the hypothesis is as follows.

Hypothesis 3 *Profit Sharing without Discretion*
$\frac{\partial (V_{01} - V_{00})}{\partial X_{j\delta}} = \beta_{\delta P} < 0$

Proposition 1 states that if the worker has decision making power, then the firm places greater value on using profit sharing when it is more difficult to monitor the worker's information. Proposition 2 states that if uncertainty has greater affect on the firm's ability to monitor than it does on the firm's profits, then the firm will use more profit sharing. In terms of the model the appropriate difference is,

$$V_{11} - V_{10} = X_{j\delta}\beta_{\delta P} + X_i\beta_{iP} + X_j\beta_{jP} \\ + X_{j\delta}\beta_{\delta DP} + X_i\beta_{iDP} + X_j\beta_{jDP} + \epsilon_{ijP} + \epsilon_{ijDP} \quad (12)$$

Therefore, the propositions imply the following hypothesis. The hypothesis states that conditional on the worker having decision making power and assuming uncertainty has greater impact on the firm's ability to monitor, greater uncertainty increases the latent profits of using profit sharing.

Hypothesis 4 *Profit Sharing with Discretion*
$\frac{\partial(V_{11}-V_{10})}{\partial X_{j\delta}} = \beta_{\delta P} + \beta_{\delta DP} > 0$

If we also that variation in firm profits has the same effect on the incentive problem, irrespective of whether the agent has discretion, then $\beta_{\delta P}$ will account for this variation in firm profits. This means that $\beta_{\delta DP}$ will measure the effect of uncertainty on the ability of the firm to monitor the worker's private information. Under this assumption, if Hypothesis 4 holds, $\beta_{\delta DP} > \beta_{\delta P}$, suggesting that uncertainty has a greater impact on the firm's ability to monitor than it does on firm profits. If the hypothesis does not hold then uncertainty has a greater impact on firm profits than on the ability of the firm to monitor the worker's information. Under this assumption the test of the model is whether $\beta_{\delta DP} > 0$.

The hypotheses are tested on a data set based on a large survey of employees in British manufacturing. The next section discusses the data.

3 Data

The sample is based on Workplace Employee Relations Survey (WERS) 1998 and includes information on workers in private manufacturing firms. The sample uses information collected from 247 managers or senior administrators and 1,358 production line workers in 166 private sector manufacturing establishments.[6] For a more detailed description of the sample see Adams (2003).[7]

The analysis uses two dependent variables: whether decision making power is delegated to the worker and the type of contract offered to the worker. Both are dichotomous variables. The variable DECISION MAKING is 1 if the worker states that he has influence over the range of tasks that he performs, and 0 otherwise.[8] This measure does not vary with the degree of decision making power, rather it simply measures whether the worker has any sort of decision making power over the tasks he performs (from "a little" to a "a lot"). The theory makes substantially different predictions depending on whether the worker has discretion or not, the amount of discretion does not seem to be as important.

The variable PROFIT SHARING is 1 if the employee's firm offers either profit sharing or share ownership to that type of employee, and 0 otherwise. For production workers it is 1 if more than 80 % of its non-managerial employees including its operators, assembly workers or skilled trades persons (depending on the self-description of the worker), and 0 if less than 20 % of it's non-managerial employees have profit sharing or share ownership.[9] A concern with PROFIT SHARING is that it is not based on a direct response by the employee, but rather it is based on a series of questions given to the firm. Therefore the probability that an employee receives profit sharing is not independent across members of the same firm.[10] Also, there is a possibil-

---

[6]Because of missing variables, the exact numbers will differ between regressions.

[7]For a more detailed description of the survey, see Cully et al. (1999).

[8]The question states 'In general, how much influence do you have about the following? The range of tasks you do in your job ("A lot", "Some", "A little", "None", "Don't know")' (Department of Trade and Industry, Advisory, Conciliation and Arbitration Service (2000)).

[9]Profit sharing and share ownership are two different schemes that are combined in the analysis. For a discussion and analysis of the differences between the two schemes see Jones and Pliskin (1997).

[10]This correlation is accounted for in the empirical results presented in Section 4.

ity that an employee is coded as having profit sharing but actually does not. This would occur when more than 80 % of the non-managerial employees in the worker's establishment have profit sharing but the particular is not part of the 80 % that receive it. Similarly, there is a possibility that an employee is coded as *not* having profit sharing when he actually does if less than 20 % of non-managerial employees in the establishment have profit sharing but he is a member of the small fraction that do.[11]

There are three measures to describe the firm's product market. The first measure is CHANGING which is 1 if the manager stated that the market for the firm's main product is not stable, and is set to 0 otherwise.[12] This measure attempts to capture both the amount of volatility there may be in the profits of the firm, as well as the amount of uncertainty there is in the information available to the worker's supervisor. The second measure is MULTI-PRODUCT which is 1 if the establishment produces multiple products, and 0 otherwise. This measure is meant to complement CHANGING by measuring the amount of volatility there is on the production floor. The expectation is that firms that produce multiple products will be more likely to change the types of orders that are on the production line, which may increase the amount of uncertainty in monitoring the worker's decisions.[13] The third measure of the firm's product market is QUALITY, which is 1 if the manager stated that the firm has achieved some externally assessed quality standard, and 0 otherwise. The literature suggests that it will be more difficult to monitor the worker's actions when those actions include quality margins as well as quantity margins (Drago and Heywood (1995); Holmstrom

---

[11]Employees in establishments which state that between 20 % and 80 % of employees have profit sharing are dropped from the sample. This criteria has little effect on results and only a small number of firms are eliminated from the data set.

[12]The question states 'which of these statements best describes the current state of the market for the establishment's main product? ("the market is growing," "the market is mature," "the market is declining," "the market is turbulent")' (Department of Trade and Industry, Advisory, Conciliation and Arbitration Service (2000)).

[13]I also run the analysis with a more restrictive definition of CHANGING, that is 1 if the market is "turbulent," and 0 otherwise. While the resulting coefficients have the same size, they are generally not statistically significant.

and Milgrom (1991); Prendergast (1999)).

The analysis uses one measure of the firm's characteristics, SIZE which is measured by the total number of full-time employees in the workplace. Previous studies have shown the size of the firm to be an important determinant of both the degree to which decision making power is delegated to the shopfloor (Adams (2001); Osterman (1994)) and the degree to which profit sharing is used (Adams (2002a); Jones and Pliskin (1997)). The incentive literature suggests that when there are more workers covered by a particular incentive scheme there is more likely to be "shirking" or free-riding (Holmstrom (1982)).[14]

The analysis uses four measures of employee characteristics. The first, 2YEARS is 1 if the worker has been at the firm for more than 2 years, and 0 otherwise. This measure is meant to capture the worker's knowledge and experience with the production process. It is expected to be an important determinant of worker discretion (Adams (2003)). The second, UNION MEMBER, is 1 if the employee is a member of a union and 0 otherwise. Previous work suggests that the existence of unions decreases the likelihood that the firm will delegate decision making power to production workers (Adams (2001); Osterman (1994)). It has also been argued that unions tend to be opposed to profit sharing (Gregg and Marchin (1988)). However, a firm may have greater difficulty disciplining or firing a union member than a non-union member. After all that is one reason employees join unions! The *a priori* "union effect" could positively or negatively effect the probability that the worker receives profit sharing. The third characteristic, MALE is 1 if the employee is male and 0 if the employee is female. The fourth and final characteristic of the employee, SKILLED is 1 if the employee is a skilled trades person and 0 if the employee is an operator or assembly worker. One concern with the measure DECISION MAKING, is that it may vary systematically across types of work. Though more detail would be preferred, SKILLED is the only measure of the type of work available in the data set. However, this measure may not be exogenous because firms can choose the skill of the

---

[14]This issue is the subject of a recent paper by the author (Adams (2002a)).

Variable	*Manager*	*Worker*
Decision Making	1.00	.77
Profit Sharing	.62	.47
Decision Making and Profit Sharing	.62	.37
Changing	.64	.64
Multiple Products	.64	.54
Size - Number of Full-Time Workers	542 (1535)	428 (1182)
Quality	.72	.71
Union Member	.15	.55
Male	.89	.77
Two Years Experience	.87	.83
Skilled	-	.39
Number in Sample	247	1358

Table 3: Sample Frequencies by Employee Type (standard deviation)

worker. If there are unmeasured characteristics of the firm that determine both the skill level of a particular employee and whether the worker will be given DECISION MAKING, then using this measure could bias estimates.[15]

Table 3 presents the unweighted sample frequencies of the variables used in the analysis. The first column presents the frequencies as a percentage of the managers and the second column presents the frequencies as a percentage of the workers. Almost 100 % of the managers and 77 % of workers have (some) decision making power over the tasks they perform,[16] 62 % and 47 % respectively, have profit sharing or share ownership and 62 % and 32 % respectively, have both decision making and profit sharing. 64 % of the managers and the workers are in firms that face changing markets.

---

[15] The results presented below include SKILLED as an explanatory variable. Dropping this variable and (separately) restricting the sample to unskilled workers (operators and assembly workers) does not have a significant effect on the main results of the paper.

[16] 1 of the 247 managers claims not have decision making power.

4 Results

The results presented in Table 4 provides some initial support for Hypotheses 3 and 4. The table presents two sets of probit regressions on weighted data. The first is run on managers and senior administrators in manufacturing firms. The second is run on production workers in manufacturing firms. If it is the case that managers are agents with discretion and workers are agents without discretion, then there is some empirical support for Hypotheses 3 and 4. In particular,

$$\beta_{\delta P} = -.26 < 0 \tag{13}$$

which is the coefficient on CHANGING in the regression on production workers (column 3). This coefficient is of the hypothesized sign, but is not statistically significantly different from 0. Also,

$$\beta_{\delta P} + \beta_{\delta DP} = .45 > 0 \tag{14}$$

which is the coefficient on CHANGING in the regression on managers (column 2). This coefficient is the hypothesized sign but is not statistically different from 0. Note that this regression does not allow us to separately estimate $\beta_{\delta DP}$. Although the results are not strong, they are suggestive, and they are of the predicted sign.

A concern with the regression presented on the workers is that some workers may actually have discretion, and this may be biasing the results. Table 5 presents probit regressions for workers with and without discretion.[17] The results give support for Hypothesis 3, which states that for workers without discretion the more uncertainty the less use of profit sharing there will be. In particular,

$$\beta_{\delta P} = -.59 < 0 \tag{15}$$

which is the coefficient on CHANGING in the regression on production workers with "No Discretion" (column 2). The coefficient is the hypothesized sign and statistically significantly different from 0 (p value = .066). For the mean

---

[17]Note that because of the smaller sample size, the variables MALE, SKILLED, and 2YEARS are dropped.

	Managers		Workers	
	β	% Δ	β	% Δ
Changing	.45	.18	-.26	-.10
	(.32)	(.12)	(.27)	(.11)
Size	-.0002	-.00007	-.0002	-.00006
	(.0001)	(.00003)	(.0001)	(.00003)
Male	-.08	-.03	.16	.06
	(.29)	(.11)	(.21)	(.08)
2Years	.10	.04	-.02	-.01
	(.33)	(.13)	(.17)	(.07)
Skilled	-	-	.03	.01
			(.18)	(.07)
Quality	.38	.15	.34	.13
	(.34)	(.13)	(.28)	(.10)
Union	-.69	-.27	.33	.13
	(.33)	(.12)	(.21)	(.08)
Multiproduct	-.45	-.17	.00	.00
	(.34)	(.12)	(.25)	(.10)
Constant	.35		-.41	
	(.51)		(.37)	
Log Likelihood	-121.10		-686.53	
Sample Size	227		1,100	

Table 4: Probit Regressions on Profit Sharing (Robust Standard Errors)

	No Discretion		Discretion	
	β	% Δ	β	% Δ
Changing	-.59	-.22	-.10	-.04
	(.32)	(.12)	(.27)	(.11)
Size	-.00011	-.00004	-.0002	-.00008
	(.00005)	(.00002)	(.0001)	(.00003)
Quality	.07	.03	.44	.17
	(.37)	(.14)	(.29)	(.10)
Union	.15	.06	.37	.14
	(.26)	(.10)	(.21)	(.08)
Multiproduct	-.21	-.08	.04	.02
	(.31)	(.12)	(.25)	(.10)
Constant	.19		-.45	
	(.38)		(.34)	
Log Likelihood	-150.12		-523.08	
Sample Size	248		835	

Table 5: Probits on Worker Profit Sharing (Robust Standard Errors)

worker without discretion, the existence of changing demand leads to a 22 percentage point reduction in the probability of having profit sharing. The results presented in Tables 4 and 5 show the importance of accounting for discretion in empirically testing the relationship between risk and incentives. For workers without discretion, the theory is supported.

These results presented in Table 5 do not provide support for Hypothesis 4. The inequality is,

$$\beta_{\delta P} + \beta_{\delta DP} = -.10 < 0 \qquad (16)$$

which is the coefficient on CHANGING in the regression on workers with discretion (column 3). This coefficient is *not* the hypothesized sign and is not statistically different from 0. Note that this regression also does not allow us to separately estimate $\beta_{\delta DP}$. The following estimator allows all the parameters to be estimated separately and assumes that the choice of the firm to give the worker discretion and profit sharing are made simultaneously and these choices interact. The estimator is described in detail in Adams (2003, 2002b).[18]

The results presented in Table 6 provide support for three of the four hypotheses. Hypothesis 1 states that the value of discretion and profit sharing is increasing with uncertainty. The inequality is

$$\beta_{\delta D} + \beta_{\delta P} + \beta_{\delta DP} = -.05 - 1.08 + 2.67 = 1.54 > 0 \qquad (17)$$

The inequality is of the hypothesized sign and is statistically significantly different from 0. Hypothesis 3 states that conditional on the worker having no discretion, the value of profit sharing decreases with uncertainty. From Table 6,

$$\beta_{\delta P} = -1.08 < 0 \qquad (18)$$

The estimated coefficient is the hypothesized sign and is statistically different from 0. Hypothesis 4 states that conditional on the worker having decision making power, the value of profit sharing will increase with uncertainty.

$$\beta_{\delta P} + \beta_{\delta DP} = -1.08 + 2.67 = 1.59 > 0 \qquad (19)$$

---

[18] A similar model is discussed in Greene (2000).

Variable	β	Robust SE
Decision Making (β_D)		
Changing	-.05	(.14)
Quality	-.05	(.12)
2 Years	.27	(.13)
Skilled	.09	(.11)
Union Member	-.21	(.10)
Constant	.63	(.17)
Profit Sharing (β_P)		
Changing	-1.08	(.22)
Multi-Product	.11	(.09)
Size	-.00010	(.00004)
Quality	.01	(.35)
Union Member	.19	(.12)
Constant	-.03	(.35)
Interaction (β_{DP})		
Changing	2.67	(.76)
Quality	.23	(.41)
Constant	-1.93	(.92)
ρ_{12}	-.25	(.08)
ρ_{13}	.21	(.16)
ρ_{23}	-.96	(.04)
Log likelihood	-2,178.95	
Number	1,083	

Table 6: Simultaneous Model for Workers

The sum of the estimated coefficients is the hypothesized sign and is statistically different from 0. These results are consistent with the theory presented above. At the very least, the results show the importance of accounting for discretion in analyzing the use of performance based pay schemes.

Hypothesis 2 is not supported by the results. The hypothesis states that giving the worker decision making and profit sharing is *complementary*. In the estimated model the negative coefficient on the constant term implies that for some workers the two practices are independent of each other (the firm's value of the two practices is not supermodular) (Adams (2002b, 2003)). The positive coefficient on other terms, means that for other firms these two practices are complements. In particular, the two practices are more likely to be complements for firms with changing demand.

If it is the case that variation in firm profits affects the incentive problem in the same manner, irrespective of agent discretion, then the effect of uncertainty on firm profits is captured by the $\beta_{\delta P}$ term. The effect of uncertainty on the ability of the firm to monitor the worker's private information is captured by the $\beta_{\delta DP}$ term. Equation (19) shows that $\beta_{\delta DP} > \beta_{\delta P}$, suggesting that uncertainty affects the firm's ability to monitor the worker's information more than it affects variation in firm profits.

The results are consistent with previous work. If the worker is a member of the union then he is *less* likely to be given decision making power. The result is consistent with the general findings about the use of employee involvement programs such as self-managed work teams. Firms with unions tend to be less likely to adopt such programs and are less likely delegate greater decision making power to the shop floor (Adams (2001); Osterman (1994)). This result goes further by stating that even within firms, individual union members are less likely to get decision making power. On the use of profit sharing schemes, the results suggest that firms that produce high quality products are more likely to use profit sharing (Drago and Heywood (1995)).[19]

---

[19] Note however that the coefficients on QUALITY are not statistically significant.

5 Conclusion

A fundamental tenet of incentive theory is a negative relationship between risk and incentives (Holmstrom (1979); Shavell (1979)). An implication is that, for example, the proportion of CEO compensation that varies with firm profits decreases as the amount of variation in firm profits increases. This occurs because variation in firm profits exposes the CEO to greater risk, and therefore the CEO needs to be paid more to accept the contract. However, there is little empirical support for such a relationship (Prendergast (1999)). A recent explanation is that there is a "missing variable bias" in data based on CEO contracts (Ackerberg and Botticini (2002); Prendergast (2002b,a); Serfes (2002)). One example of a missing variable is that CEOs are given a substantial amount of discretion in the tasks that they do and the choices they make. This paper shows that giving an agent discretion substantially alters the incentive problem. The paper shows that for agents that do not have discretion, there is a negative relationship between uncertainty and the use of profit sharing. While for agents *with* discretion, the paper shows that there is a *positive* relationship. If the agent has discretion and private information about the value of his choices, then the principal needs to know *why* actions were chosen even if they know *what* actions were chosen. There is an adverse selection problem. If uncertainty is associated with a reduction in the principal's information about "why", then the theoretical model presented above shows that uncertainty will be positively associated with the use of profit sharing.

The paper uses recently available information on the use of incentive contracts in British manufacturing firms. The data includes information on individual employees and the firms that the employees work for. In particular, the data provides proxies for the amount uncertainty that there is in the environment and for whether or not individual employees have discretion in their jobs. The empirical results support the hypothesis based on Holmstrom (1979) and Shavell (1979) that for agents without discretion there is a negative relationship between uncertainty and the use of profit sharing. The empirical results also support the hypothesis based on the theoretical model presented above, that for agents with discretion, uncertainty reduces the principal's ability to monitor the agent's information leading to greater use of profit sharing. The empirical results give mixed support for the hypotheses based on Prendergast (2002a). The results support the notion that uncertainty leads to an increased propensity to give the agent both discretion and profit sharing. However, the results do not support the notion that profit sharing must be used when the agent has discretion. Unfortunately, the data is not detailed enough to test the implications of the model presented in Core and Qian (2001). This model states that for agents with discretion, increased uncertainty increases the value of the agent's private information, and higher powered incentives are necessary to get the agent to collect this information.

The initial part of the empirical section analyzes the firm's propensity to use profit sharing conditional on whether the employee is a manager or a production worker. The assumption is that managers are likely to have discretion in their work, while production workers are not likely to have discretion. The results show that for managers there is a positive relationship between the use of profit sharing and the amount of uncertainty in the environment. However, for workers there is a negative relationship. While the statistical results aren't particulary strong, they give some support for the hypotheses. When the sample is further restricted to workers that do not have discretion, there is support for the predicted negative relationship between uncertainty and profit sharing. The empirical section also analyzes the firm's joint decision to give discretion and profit sharing to production workers. This analysis is similar to the work of Nagar (2002) on the decision to give bank managers discretion and give them performance based pay. When workers don't have discretion, the use of profit sharing decreases with the amount of uncertainty, supporting the major tenet of incentive theory. When workers have discretion, the use of profit sharing increases with the uncertainty. The empirical results are consistent with a major tenet of agency theory and are consistent with the notion that agent discretion creates an adverse selection problem that may be best solved by using profit sharing.

6 Appendix

Proof of Proposition 1. First note that V_{11} is constant in ϕ. The rest of the step shows that V_{10} increases in ϕ. By maximization any decision making contract will specify that $t(0) = 0$ and $t(1) = 1$. Given that $\sigma > 0.5$, the alternative will have lower expected revenue than a non-decision making contract. The contract must satisfy the incentive compatibility constraint.

$$(1-\phi \cdot f_1)v(\pi(1,0))+\phi \cdot f_1 v(\pi(1,1))-e \geq \phi \cdot f_1 v(\pi(0,1))+(1-\phi \cdot f_1)v(\pi(0,0)) \quad (20)$$

and

$$\phi \cdot f_0 v(\pi(0,1))+(1-\phi \cdot f_0)v(\pi(0,0)) \geq (1-\phi \cdot f_0)v(pi(1,0))+\phi \cdot f_0 v(\pi(1,1))-e \quad (21)$$

By maximization, $\pi(0,1) = \pi(0,0) = 0$ and the Equation (20) holds with equality.

$$v(\pi(1,1)) - v(\pi(1,0)) = \frac{e}{2\phi \cdot f_1 - 1} \quad (22)$$

and as $f_1 > f_0$ ($\sigma > 0.5$), Equation (21) also holds. By Equation (22) the difference $v(\pi(1,1)) - v(\pi(1,0))$ decreases as ϕ increases. Using the individual rationality constraint it is then straight forward to show that the firm's expected payment to the worker decreases as the difference $v(\pi(1,1)) - v(\pi(1,0))$ decreases. QED.

Proof of Proposition 2

1. From Equation (3) the incentive compatibility constraints are

$$(1-p_0)v(\pi(0))+p_0 v(\pi(1)) \geq (1-f_0 \cdot p_1)v(\pi(0))+f_0 \cdot p_1 v(\pi(1))-e \quad (23)$$

and

$$(1-f_1 \cdot p_1)v(\pi(0))+f_1 \cdot p_1 v(\pi(1))-e \geq (1-p_0)v(\pi(0))+p_0 v(\pi(1)) \quad (24)$$

Following the procedure used in the proof of Proposition 1, we have

$$v(\pi(1)) - v(\pi(0)) = \frac{e}{f_1 \cdot p_1 - p_0} \quad (25)$$

Noting that expected returns remain unchanged by assumption, the appropriate inequality is

$$2\phi \cdot f_1 - 1 \geq f_1 \cdot p_1 - p_0 \qquad (26)$$

using the definitions (Equations (5) and (6)), the inequality is

$$\alpha\delta \geq \beta\delta \qquad (27)$$

2. Follows from (1). QED.

References

Ackerberg, Daniel A. and Maristella Botticini, "Endogenous Matching adn the Empirical Determinants of Contract Form," *Journal of Political Economy*, June 2002, *110* (3), 564–592.

Adams, Christopher P., "Theory and Practice of Shopfloor Decision Making in Manufacturing." PhD dissertation, University of Wisconsin–Madison 2001.

_ , "Does Size Really Matter? Empirical evidence on group incentives.," July 2002. Bureau of Economics, Federal Trade Commission.

_ , "Selection of "High Performance Work Practices" in U.S. Manufacturing," March 2002. FTC Working Paper 247.

_ , "The Use of Profit Sharing When Workers Make Decisions: Evidence from a Survey of Manufacturing Workers," in Jeffrey Pliskin and Takao Kato, eds., *The Determinants of the Incidence and the Effects of Participatory Organizations*, Vol. 7, Elsevier, 2003, pp. 173–209.

Aggarwal, Rajesh K. and Andrew A. Samwick, "The Other Side of the Tradeoff: The Impact of Risk on Executive Compensation," *Journal of Political Economy*, 1999, *107*, 65–105.

_ and _ , "The Other Side of the Tradeoff: The Impact of Risk on Executive Compensation - A Reply," October 2002. Tuck School of Business, Dartmouth.

Core, John and Jun Qian, "Project Selection, Production, Uncertainty, and Incentives," November 2001. Wharton School, University of Pennsylvania.

_ **and Wayne Guay**, "The Other Side of the Trade-Off: The Impact of Risk on Executive Compensation. A Comment.," *Journal of Political Economy*, 2002, *Forthcoming*.

Cully, Mark, Stephen Woodland, Andrew O'Reilly, and Gill Dix, *Britain at Work: As Depicted by the 1998 Workplace Employee Relations Survey*, London: Routledge, 1999.

Department of Trade and Industry, Advisory, Conciliation and Arbitration Service, "Workplace Employee Relations Survey: Cross Section 1998," Computer File April 2000. 5th Edition. Colchester, Essex: The Data Archive [distributor]. SN: 3955.

Drago, Robert and John Heywood, "The Choice of Payment Schemes: Australian Establishment Data," *Industrial Relations*, 1995, *34*, 507–531.

Greene, William, *Econometric Analysis*, fourth ed., Prentice Hall, 2000.

Gregg, P. A. and S. J. Marchin, "Unions and the incidence of performance linked pay schemes in Britain," *International Journal of Industrial Organization*, 1988, *6*, 91–107.

Holmstrom, Bengt, "Moral Hazard and Observability," *Bell Journal of Economics*, 1979, *10* (1), 74–91.

_ , "Moral Hazard in Teams," *Bell Journal of Economics*, 1982.

_ **and Paul Milgrom**, "Multitask Principal-Agent Analyses: Incentive Contracts, Asset Ownership, and Job Design," *Journal of Law, Economics, and Organization*, 1991, *7*, 24–52.

Jones, Derek and Jeffrey Pliskin, "Determinants of the Incidence of Group Incentives: Evidence from Canada," *Canadian Journal of Economics*, November 1997, *30* (4b), 1027–1045.

Milgrom, Paul and John Roberts, "The Economics of Modern Manufacturing: Technology, Strategy, and Organization," *The American Economic Review*, June 1990, pp. 511–528.

Myerson, Roger, "Optimal Coordination Mechanisms in Generalized Principal-Agent Problems," *Journal of Mathematical Economics*, 1982, pp. 67–81.

_ , *Social Goals and Social Organization*, Cambridge University Press,

Nagar, Venky, "Delegation and Incentive Compensation," *The Accounting Review*, 2002, *77* (2), 379–395.

Osterman, Paul, "How Common is Workplace Transformation and Who Adopts It?," *Industrial and Labor Relations Review*, 1994, *47*, 173–187.

Oyer, Paul, "Why Do Firms Use Incentives That Have No Incentive Effects?," June 2002. Stanford University.

Prendergast, Canice, "The Provision of Incentives in Firms," *Journal of Economic Literature*, 1999, *37*, 7–63.

_ , "The Tenuous Tradeoff Between Risk and Incentives," *Journal of Political Economy*, 2002, *Forthcoming*.

_ , "Uncertainty and Incentives," *Journal of Labor Economics*, 2002, *20* (2), S115–S137.

Serfes, Konstantinos, "Risk Sharing Versus Incentives: Contract Design Under Two-Sided Heterogeneity," February 2002. Stony Brook.

Shavell, S, "Risk Sharing and Incentives in the Principal and Agent Relationship," *Bell Journal of Economics*, 1979, *10* (1), 55–73.

www.ingramcontent.com/pod-product-compliance
Lightning Source LLC
Chambersburg PA
CBHW081814170526

45167CB00008B/3433